AI for Real Estate, Crypto & Investment Taxes

AI Personal Tax Optimization: How Artificial Intelligence Helps You Keep More of What You Earn

By Joe Correa

Published by Live Stronger Faster

This book is for educational and informational purposes only. The author and publisher are not engaged in rendering legal, financial, tax, or other professional advice. Readers should consult a qualified professional before making any financial decisions.

First Edition

Table of Contents

Introduction

Modern wealth is no longer built from a single paycheck. It flows from rental properties, Airbnb income, stock portfolios, private equity, crypto wallets, NFTs, staking rewards, dividends, options trades, REITs, syndications, and digital assets that cross borders in seconds. For investors, this explosion of opportunity has created unprecedented earning power — but it has also created unprecedented tax complexity. Every trade, every rental expense, every depreciation schedule, every token swap, every capital gain, every loss harvest, and every international transaction carries tax consequences that can either drain your wealth or protect it. For decades, only hedge funds, institutional investors, and ultra-high-net-worth families had the systems and professionals needed to track and optimize this level of complexity. Today, artificial intelligence gives those same tools to everyday investors, landlords, crypto traders, and entrepreneurs — turning tax chaos into a precision-engineered wealth machine.

This book exists because real estate and investing taxes are where fortunes are either multiplied or silently destroyed. Two investors can earn the exact same income and end the year with radically different net worths simply because one used optimized tax strategy while the other relied on manual spreadsheets, basic tax software, or an overwhelmed accountant. Real estate depreciation alone can eliminate tens of thousands of dollars in taxes per year. Crypto tax loss harvesting can wipe out capital gains. Opportunity zone strategies can defer taxes for decades. Like a hidden dimension of investing, tax optimization determines whether your portfolio compounds or leaks value. Artificial intelligence does not just record these opportunities — it actively finds, models, and executes them with machine-level precision.

The traditional approach to investment taxes is backward-looking. Most people hand their documents to a CPA after the year is over and hope for the best. By that point, most tax-saving decisions are already lost forever. AI flips this model completely. It turns taxes into a real-time, forward-looking optimization engine. Every trade you consider, every property you buy, every refinance, every crypto swap, every dividend, and every sale can be simulated instantly before you execute it. AI can calculate the exact tax outcome of each option, compare strategies, and recommend the one that maximizes after-tax wealth — not just raw profit. This transforms investing from a gamble into a data-driven financial engineering system.

Real estate is one of the most powerful tax-advantaged wealth vehicles ever created, but only when its complexity is properly managed. Depreciation schedules, cost segregation, passive activity rules, 1031 exchanges, bonus depreciation, qualified business income deductions, rental loss limitations, and local tax rules create a maze that most investors barely understand. Artificial intelligence can map that maze in seconds. It reads property records, closing statements, rent rolls, expense categories, and loan documents. It builds full depreciation schedules, identifies acceleration opportunities, detects errors, and models future tax impacts. What once required teams of accountants and weeks of analysis is now handled instantly — and continuously — by AI systems that never forget a single dollar.

Crypto and digital assets add an entirely new layer of complexity that overwhelms traditional tax methods. Every token swap, liquidity pool, staking reward, NFT mint, bridge transfer, and wallet movement creates taxable events across multiple jurisdictions. Even sophisticated traders struggle to track thousands of micro-transactions across exchanges and blockchains. AI thrives in this environment. It reads blockchain ledgers directly, reconstructs transaction histories, applies tax rules to every event, and produces compliant, optimized reports automatically. More importantly, it identifies strategic opportunities such as loss harvesting, timing of disposals, and offsetting gains that human traders almost always miss. Investments are no longer limited to stocks and bonds. Today's portfolios include private companies, syndications, crowdfunded real estate, royalties, intellectual property, digital assets, foreign holdings, and algorithmic trading strategies. Each asset class is governed by different tax treatments, holding period rules, reporting obligations, and optimization strategies. AI unifies all of this into a single intelligence layer that sees your entire financial ecosystem at once. Instead of treating taxes as isolated forms, AI treats them as a coordinated system designed to protect and grow wealth over decades.

This book will show you how artificial intelligence becomes your personal investment tax strategist. You will learn how AI tracks every asset, transaction, and tax rule simultaneously. You will see how algorithms automatically categorize income, apply depreciation, identify capital gains and losses, optimize holding periods, and adjust strategies based on changing laws. You will discover how real estate portfolios, crypto wallets, brokerage accounts, and private investments can all feed into one unified AI tax brain that never sleeps and never misses an opportunity.

For investors like you — especially those building income from rentals, crypto, stocks, and digital assets — this technology changes everything. You no longer need to guess which property to sell, when to realize gains, how to structure ownership, or whether to harvest losses. AI runs thousands of simulations behind the scenes, comparing every possible path and showing you the one that produces the highest long-term, after-tax net worth. This is not just tax preparation. It is wealth engineering.

Artificial intelligence also eliminates one of the greatest dangers investors face: accidental non-compliance. Crypto reporting rules, foreign account disclosures, passive loss limitations, wash sale rules, depreciation recapture, and new IRS regulations change constantly. AI systems are updated in real time as laws evolve. They automatically apply the correct treatment to each transaction and flag potential risks before they become costly problems. Instead of reacting to IRS letters months or years later, AI helps you avoid mistakes before they ever occur.

By the end of this book, you will understand how AI turns real estate, crypto, and investment taxes into a competitive advantage. You will see how wealthy families use similar systems to legally reduce taxes, accelerate cash flow, and preserve capital across generations — and how those same tools are now available to individual investors. You will learn how to connect your accounts, properties, wallets, and portfolios to AI platforms that do the heavy lifting for you, allowing you to focus on growing wealth instead of fighting paperwork.

This is the future of investing: not just buying assets, but engineering outcomes. Not just making money, but keeping it. Not just reacting to tax bills, but shaping them in advance. With artificial intelligence, every investment becomes smarter, every dollar becomes more efficient, and every decision is guided by data instead of guesswork. Welcome to the age of AI-powered real estate, crypto, and investment taxation — where your portfolio finally works as hard as you do.

Chapter 1

Why Investment Taxes Are the Greatest Hidden Wealth Lever

Investment income looks glamorous from the outside. Rental properties produce monthly cash flow, stocks pay dividends, crypto trades generate sudden spikes in account balances, and private deals promise exponential growth. But what most investors fail to realize is that the IRS quietly sits beside every one of those income streams, collecting a share of nearly every dollar that flows through them. Taxes are not a side issue in investing; they are the primary force that determines whether your portfolio compounds or stagnates. A portfolio that earns 12 percent annually but loses 40 percent of its gains to taxes will underperform a portfolio earning 8 percent with optimized tax efficiency. Wealth is built not by gross returns, but by what remains after taxes.

Most investors believe their biggest risk is market volatility. In reality, their biggest risk is tax inefficiency. When you buy or sell a rental property without planning for depreciation recapture, you may lose more than half your profit. When you trade crypto without tracking cost basis across wallets, you may pay tax on money you never actually earned. When you rebalance a portfolio without understanding capital gains timing, you may trigger unnecessary tax bills that permanently reduce your compounding power. These silent leaks add up to hundreds of thousands or even millions of dollars over a lifetime. AI exists to close those leaks.

The financial system was never designed for individuals managing dozens or hundreds of income streams. It was designed for institutions with teams of accountants, tax lawyers, and analysts. Today, an individual investor might own five rental properties, trade crypto daily, earn dividends from multiple brokerages, receive royalties, and participate in private investments — all across multiple platforms. Human accounting methods break down at this scale. AI, however, thrives on complexity. The more data you give it, the more powerful it becomes.

Artificial intelligence does not just record what happened. It understands what happened. It reads transactions, categorizes them, applies tax law, and predicts future outcomes. If you sell a property, AI instantly calculates capital gains, depreciation recapture, state taxes, and alternative strategies such as 1031 exchanges. If you trade crypto, AI tracks every token's cost basis and determines whether it qualifies for short-term or long-term treatment. If you hold investments across accounts, AI sees the entire system rather than fragmented pieces. One of the most dangerous myths in investing is that taxes are unavoidable. The truth is that tax law is a complex incentive system designed to reward certain behaviors. Real estate is rewarded with depreciation. Long-term investing is rewarded with lower capital gains rates. Opportunity zones defer taxes. Retirement accounts shelter growth. Losses can offset gains. The wealthy do not avoid taxes by breaking the law — they avoid taxes by understanding the law better than everyone else. AI gives you that same advantage.

The power of AI comes from its ability to simulate thousands of scenarios in seconds. Should you sell this property now or next year? Should you harvest crypto losses today or wait? Should you refinance or sell? Should you move assets into an LLC or keep them personally owned? Each option has a tax impact that compounds over time. Humans guess. AI calculates.

When you connect your real estate, crypto, and investment accounts to AI, it builds a living financial model of your life. It knows what you own, what you earn, how long you have held each asset, and how each tax rule applies. This allows it to identify opportunities before they disappear. It can warn you when a trade will trigger unnecessary tax. It can suggest when to realize gains. It can recommend restructuring ownership to reduce liability. This is how taxes stop being a burden and become a strategic weapon. In the past, only billionaires had access to this kind of real-time tax intelligence. Today, anyone with a smartphone can connect their financial life to AI. This democratization of financial engineering is one of the greatest wealth-building opportunities in history. It means that individuals who adopt AI early will compound faster than those who do not — regardless of starting capital.

This chapter marks the beginning of your transformation from a passive taxpayer into an active wealth optimizer. By understanding how taxes really work beneath the surface of investing, you gain control over your financial destiny. And with artificial intelligence as your partner, you are no longer limited by human error, memory, or complexity. You are operating at machine precision in a world designed for those who can see the whole board.

"The Ledger That Never Slept"

Marcus had built his fortune the hard way. Rental properties, crypto trading, dividend stocks, and a handful of private investments had turned him into a millionaire on paper. Yet every year, tax season felt like a gut punch. No matter how much he earned, the IRS always seemed to take more than he expected. He would sit at his kitchen table surrounded by statements, wallets, spreadsheets, and receipts, feeling like his money was slipping through invisible cracks. One April morning, Marcus finally snapped. His accountant handed him a six-figure tax bill and casually explained that depreciation recapture, short-term capital gains, and crypto reporting rules were the reason. Marcus realized something terrifying: he had made great investments, but terrible tax decisions. He wasn't losing to the market. He was losing to complexity.

That night, Marcus connected his accounts to an AI tax optimization platform he had heard about from a fellow investor. Within minutes, the system had ingested his entire financial life — rental income, expenses, mortgages, crypto wallets, exchange trades, dividends, and past tax returns. The dashboard came alive like a digital brain, mapping every asset and every dollar.

The next morning, Marcus saw something he had never seen before: a complete model of his wealth. The AI showed him where he was overpaying, where he was missing deductions, and where smarter timing could save him tens of thousands of dollars. It highlighted crypto losses he could harvest. It flagged a property that should be refinanced instead of sold. It recommended a 1031 exchange strategy he had never considered.

Over the next year, Marcus followed the AI's guidance. Every investment decision came with a tax forecast. Every trade was simulated before execution. Slowly, his tax bills shrank while his net worth grew. He was no longer reacting to the IRS — he was planning around it.

By the time the next tax season arrived, Marcus owed less than half of what he had paid the year before, despite earning more. For the first time, he felt in control. His wealth was no longer leaking away in silence. It was compounding, protected by a machine that never forgot, never guessed, and never slept.

And as Marcus watched his portfolio grow, he realized that the greatest investment he had ever made wasn't in property, stocks, or crypto — it was in intelligence.

Chapter 2

How AI Tracks Every Asset, Wallet, Property & Investment Automatically

The greatest weakness in traditional tax systems is fragmentation. Your rental properties live in one spreadsheet, your brokerage accounts in another, your crypto wallets in half a dozen exchanges, and your private investments in PDF statements that never quite line up. Each system sees only a piece of your financial reality. Artificial intelligence changes this by creating a single, unified financial brain that watches everything at once. It does not ask you to remember, reconcile, or re-enter data. It simply connects to your financial life and begins tracking it in real time.

When AI connects to your real estate portfolio, it reads property records, mortgage balances, rental income, repair costs, HOA fees, insurance, taxes, and depreciation schedules. It knows which properties are active, which are vacant, which are being renovated, and which are producing income. It understands cost basis, loan-to-value, and equity growth. Instead of static annual records, it creates a living digital twin of every property you own, allowing tax rules to be applied instantly and continuously. Crypto tracking is even more powerful. Every wallet, exchange, blockchain, and transaction is captured. AI reads the blockchain itself, not just exchange statements. It reconstructs your trading history across wallets, bridges, DeFi platforms, NFTs, staking protocols, and liquidity pools. It knows exactly when you acquired each token, how much you paid, how long you held it, and how it moved. This eliminates the most common cause of crypto tax disasters: missing cost basis and misclassified transactions.

Investment accounts are also brought into the same intelligence layer. Stocks, ETFs, bonds, options, dividends, interest, and private placements all flow into one model. AI tracks holding periods, dividend classifications, wash sale rules, and capital gains in real time. If you move assets between accounts or brokerages, AI follows them. It does not care where the money is stored — it cares what the money is doing.

This unified view is what gives AI its power. It can see when a crypto gain could be offset by a real estate loss. It can see when selling one asset will push you into a higher tax bracket. It can see how depreciation on one property shields income from another. Human accountants can never hold this many variables in their head. AI can hold millions.

Automation also eliminates the most dangerous enemy of tax optimization: human error. A single missed transaction, forgotten wallet, or misclassified expense can trigger audits, penalties, and lost deductions. AI does not forget. It does not get tired. It does not rely on memory. It watches every dollar move in real time and categorizes it according to the latest tax rules.

This constant tracking turns taxes into a dynamic system rather than a once-a-year nightmare. You can see your estimated tax liability every day. You can see how new investments will affect it. You can adjust your strategy before problems arise. Taxes stop being a shock and become a controllable variable.

Most importantly, AI makes complex portfolios accessible to ordinary investors. You no longer need a team of specialists to manage real estate, crypto, and investments. You only need one intelligent system that understands all of them simultaneously. That is the true revolution of AI-powered tax optimization.

"The Map of Everything"

Elena owned more assets than she could remember. Three rental properties, two Airbnbs, crypto spread across five exchanges, dividend stocks, and a small private equity stake. Every year she dreaded tax season, not because she didn't make money, but because she could never be sure where it all went.

One afternoon she connected everything to an AI tax system. At first, she expected another dashboard of numbers. Instead, what appeared on her screen looked like a living map. Every property, wallet, account, and investment was connected by flowing lines of data. It was the first time she had ever seen her financial life as a single system.

The AI showed her something shocking. One of her crypto wallets contained tokens she had forgotten about that were sitting at a large unrealized loss. At the same time, one of her rental properties was generating taxable income that could be offset by harvesting those losses. The AI recommended a simple sequence of trades and transfers that would save her over $18,000 in taxes that year.

Elena followed the plan. When tax season arrived, her bill was dramatically lower. But more importantly, she no longer felt lost. Her money was no longer scattered. It was mapped, understood, and optimized.

From that day forward, Elena never made an investment without consulting her AI. And for the first time in her life, she felt like she truly owned her wealth — instead of being owned by it.

Chapter 3

How AI Optimizes Capital Gains, Loss Harvesting & Timing

Capital gains are one of the most misunderstood forces in investing. Most investors think profit is what they make when an asset increases in value. In reality, profit is what remains after taxes. A perfectly timed sale can mean the difference between paying a short-term rate that takes nearly half of your gain and a long-term rate that allows most of it to remain in your pocket. Artificial intelligence brings precision to this timing, turning capital gains into a controllable variable instead of a dangerous surprise.

Every asset you own has a clock attached to it. Stocks, crypto, real estate, and private investments all move from short-term to long-term treatment based on holding period rules. Humans struggle to track these timelines across dozens or hundreds of positions. AI tracks them automatically, down to the second. It knows when a token, a share, or a property crosses the threshold that lowers your tax rate, and it alerts you when waiting just a little longer could save you thousands of dollars.

Loss harvesting is the hidden twin of capital gains. When assets decline in value, most investors feel only pain. AI sees opportunity. It identifies unrealized losses across your entire portfolio and determines how they can be used to offset current or future gains. A crypto crash, a down year in stocks, or a temporary dip in property values becomes a tax shield rather than a disaster. AI can even rotate investments so that you stay in the market while still realizing the loss for tax purposes.

Timing is everything. If you sell too early, you pay higher taxes. If you sell too late, you may miss a strategic offset. AI continuously models the best possible moments to act. It compares market conditions, tax brackets, income levels, and holding periods to find the window where taxes are minimized and long-term wealth is maximized. What feels like guesswork becomes math.

This optimization extends beyond individual assets. AI looks at your entire financial life. It knows when one sale will push you into a higher bracket and when spreading sales across multiple years will save you money. It understands how real estate depreciation can shelter investment gains. It coordinates every move so that no decision is made in isolation.

The result is a portfolio that compounds faster simply because fewer dollars leak away. Over a lifetime, this difference is staggering. Two investors with identical returns can end decades apart in wealth simply because one managed timing better. With AI, you always have that advantage.

"The Perfect Moment"

David was a crypto trader who lived on adrenaline. He bought low, sold high, and watched charts like a hawk. But despite his trading skill, his bank account never seemed to grow as fast as his portfolio. Taxes were eating him alive.

When he connected his accounts to an AI tax optimizer, the system showed him something he had never considered. Several of his biggest gains were taxed at the highest rate because he sold them just weeks before qualifying for long-term treatment. Meanwhile, dozens of losing trades were sitting idle, wasting their potential to offset gains.

The AI built a new plan. It told David exactly which assets to sell now, which to hold, and which losses to harvest. It even timed his trades to avoid pushing him into a higher tax bracket.

For the first time, David wasn't just trading the market – he was trading the tax code. By the end of the year, his profits were higher, but his taxes were lower. The perfect moment, he realized, wasn't when prices peaked. It was when intelligence and timing aligned.

Chapter 4

How AI Transforms Real Estate Depreciation, Cost Segregation & Passive Loss Rules

Real estate is the single most tax-advantaged asset class available to individual investors, yet it is also one of the most misunderstood. Most property owners believe depreciation is a simple annual deduction applied evenly over time. In reality, depreciation is a powerful tax-engineering tool that can be accelerated, restructured, timed, and coordinated across an entire portfolio to legally eliminate large portions of taxable income. Artificial intelligence unlocks this power by turning depreciation from a static accounting line item into a dynamic, continuously optimized strategy.

Depreciation exists because tax law recognizes that buildings wear out over time. Instead of allowing you to deduct the full cost of a property in the year you purchase it, the IRS allows that cost to be recovered gradually over a defined schedule. Residential rental property is typically depreciated over 27.5 years, while commercial property is depreciated over 39 years. On paper, this seems straightforward. In practice, it creates enormous opportunity. Not all parts of a building wear out at the same rate, and AI understands this distinction in extraordinary detail.

Cost segregation is the process of breaking a property into its individual components and depreciating them on faster schedules. Flooring, appliances, wiring, plumbing, fixtures, cabinetry, and certain structural elements can often be depreciated over 5, 7, or 15 years instead of 27.5 or 39. Traditional cost segregation studies were expensive, slow, and limited to large commercial properties. AI changes this entirely. It analyzes purchase documents, property records, construction data, and comparable studies to perform automated cost segregation at scale, making advanced depreciation strategies available to everyday investors.

Artificial intelligence does not simply apply depreciation once and forget about it. It continuously monitors your portfolio. If you renovate a property, AI adjusts the depreciation schedule. If you add a new appliance, it tracks its useful life. If tax law changes, it recalculates future deductions. This living depreciation model ensures that no deductible dollar is ever lost, delayed, or misapplied.

Passive activity loss rules are another area where most investors unknowingly lose massive tax benefits. Rental income is typically considered passive, meaning losses can be limited depending on your income level and participation status. Many investors assume that if they cannot deduct losses today, they are useless. AI understands that passive losses are not lost — they are stored. It tracks suspended losses across properties and years, waiting for the precise moment they can be unleashed to offset future income or capital gains.

AI also understands when real estate losses can offset active income. Real estate professionals, short-term rental operators, and investors who meet material participation thresholds can often deduct losses against non-passive income. Determining eligibility is complex and often misunderstood. AI analyzes your activity patterns, time logs, rental duration, and income sources to determine whether you qualify — and it documents the evidence automatically.

The coordination between depreciation and capital gains is where AI becomes truly transformative. When you sell a property, depreciation recapture can create a significant tax bill if not properly planned. AI models this years in advance. It compares selling versus refinancing. It evaluates 1031 exchanges. It determines whether holding longer, exchanging, or restructuring ownership will minimize lifetime tax exposure. These are decisions that must be made before the sale, not after. AI ensures you never miss that window. Perhaps most importantly, AI integrates real estate depreciation with the rest of your financial life. It knows when rental losses can offset crypto gains. It knows when depreciation can shelter dividend income. It knows how selling one property will affect the tax treatment of another. Instead of treating each property as a standalone asset, AI treats your entire portfolio as a single, optimized system.

This is why wealthy investors rarely fear taxes. Their real estate portfolios are not just producing income — they are producing tax shields. Artificial intelligence brings this same level of sophistication to individual investors, transforming real estate from a cash-flow tool into a long-term wealth preservation engine.

By the end of this chapter, you should understand that depreciation is not a technical detail. It is a strategic weapon. And with AI managing it continuously, intelligently, and legally, your real estate portfolio becomes one of the most powerful tax-optimization tools you will ever own.

"The House That Paid for Everything"

When Victor bought his first rental property, he thought he understood real estate. The numbers worked. The rent covered the mortgage. There was a little cash flow left over each month. To him, that was success. What he did not understand was that the true value of the property had nothing to do with rent checks. It had everything to do with what happened behind the scenes, where taxes quietly determined whether his efforts would lead to freedom or frustration.

For the first three years, Victor's tax returns looked the same. He reported rental income, deducted expenses, and paid whatever his accountant told him to pay. Depreciation appeared as a single line item, something he barely noticed. When he complained about taxes, his accountant shrugged and said, "That's just how it works." Victor accepted this as truth, never realizing how much money he was leaving on the table.

Everything changed when Victor bought his second property, a small duplex. This time, a fellow investor suggested he connect his properties to an AI tax optimization platform. Victor expected little more than automation. What he got was a revelation.

The AI didn't just record his properties — it dissected them. It read his closing documents. It analyzed construction dates, materials, and layouts. It broke each property into dozens of components, assigning accelerated depreciation schedules where legally allowed. Overnight, Victor's depreciation deductions tripled.

The first tax projection stunned him. His rental income was now almost entirely shielded. But that was only the beginning. The AI showed him that his suspended losses from prior years were stacking up quietly in the background, waiting for the right moment. It showed him that a future sale could trigger depreciation recapture — or be avoided entirely with a properly timed exchange.

As months passed, Victor trusted the system more. When he renovated a kitchen, the AI adjusted depreciation automatically. When he replaced an HVAC unit, it tracked the write-off. When he considered selling one property, the AI modeled three different futures: sell now and pay heavily, refinance and defer, or exchange and compound. Each scenario came with exact tax outcomes projected years into the future.

Then the unexpected happened. Victor made a large profit trading crypto during a volatile market cycle. He braced himself for a brutal tax bill. Instead, the AI calmly showed him how accumulated real estate losses and accelerated depreciation would offset most of the gains. What he thought would cost him six figures in taxes barely registered.

That year, Victor paid less tax than he had paid when he owned just one property — despite earning far more. His real estate wasn't just producing income anymore. It was paying for his investments, his mistakes, and his growth. Years later, when Victor finally sold one of his properties through a carefully structured exchange, he realized something profound. That house had paid for everything – not just with rent, but with intelligence. Not through luck, but through strategy. And the silent partner behind it all was a system that never slept, never forgot, and never let a dollar go to waste.

Chapter 5

How AI Coordinates Real Estate, Crypto & Investments Into One Tax Strategy

Most investors manage assets in isolation. Real estate lives in one mental box, crypto in another, stocks and investments in another, and taxes in a completely separate category altogether. This fragmented thinking is the single greatest reason investors overpay taxes year after year. Artificial intelligence changes the game by collapsing every asset class into one coordinated system. Instead of asking, "How is this property taxed?" or "How are my crypto gains taxed?" AI asks a far more powerful question: "How should all of these assets work together to minimize lifetime taxes and maximize long-term wealth?"

Tax law was never designed to treat assets independently. It is a web of interactions, offsets, thresholds, timing rules, and incentives. A gain in one area can be neutralized by a loss in another. Depreciation in real estate can shield profits from stocks or crypto. Capital losses can be carried forward to future years. Passive losses can accumulate and detonate at the right moment. Humans struggle to coordinate these moving parts because they unfold over years or decades. AI excels precisely because it can see across time. Artificial intelligence builds a unified tax architecture that spans your entire financial life. It understands how your rental properties, short-term rentals, crypto trades, dividend income, interest income, and private investments interact within the same tax return. It does not simply react to events — it plans them. Every decision is evaluated not only for its immediate profit but for its downstream tax impact across multiple years.

One of AI's most powerful capabilities is tax synchronization. Instead of allowing gains and losses to occur randomly, AI aligns them intentionally. It may recommend harvesting crypto losses in a year when real estate income is high. It may recommend delaying a property sale until depreciation has fully offset accumulated gains elsewhere. It may suggest accelerating deductions during high-income years and deferring income into lower-tax periods. This orchestration transforms taxes from an annual chore into a strategic rhythm.

AI also understands tax brackets in a way humans rarely do. Many investors unknowingly push themselves into higher brackets by stacking gains in a single year. AI continuously monitors your projected taxable income and adjusts strategies to keep you within optimal ranges. It spreads gains across years when possible, times income recognition, and ensures that deductions are used when they create the most impact. This alone can preserve enormous amounts of capital over time. Coordination becomes even more critical as portfolios grow. Investors with multiple properties, active trading strategies, and diverse investments often reach a point where their tax situation feels uncontrollable. AI thrives in this environment. It does not become overwhelmed as complexity increases — it becomes more accurate. The more assets you own, the more opportunities AI finds to offset, shelter, and optimize.

Another overlooked advantage of AI coordination is risk reduction. When assets are managed independently, investors often violate tax rules without realizing it. Wash sales, passive loss limitations, misclassified income, and reporting errors occur silently. AI detects these risks before they materialize. It flags conflicts between strategies and adjusts plans to remain compliant while still maximizing efficiency. This proactive compliance protects wealth just as much as deductions do.

Perhaps the most profound shift AI creates is psychological. Investors stop fearing taxes. They stop dreading large gains. They stop delaying opportunities because they are unsure of the consequences. With AI providing clarity, confidence replaces anxiety. Every decision is backed by data, simulation, and foresight. Taxes no longer dictate behavior — strategy does.

By coordinating real estate, crypto, and investments into a single intelligent tax strategy, AI allows wealth to compound uninterrupted. Instead of leaking value at every turn, your portfolio becomes a closed system where dollars are recycled, preserved, and reinvested with maximum efficiency. This is how long-term wealth is built quietly, legally, and sustainably.

This chapter marks the moment where individual optimization becomes system-wide mastery. When AI is allowed to see everything at once, taxes cease to be a burden and become an invisible ally — shaping outcomes in your favor year after year.

"The Year Everything Finally Clicked"

When Sarah looked back at her financial life, it felt like a series of disconnected wins and losses. One year, real estate did well but taxes were brutal. Another year, crypto exploded but wiped out her cash reserves when the tax bill arrived. Stocks paid dividends that felt nice until April came around. She was making money, but it never seemed to stay.

Sarah was not reckless. She was organized, diligent, and disciplined. But she managed each asset in isolation, trusting that things would somehow balance out. They never did.

The year everything changed began quietly. Sarah connected her rental properties, brokerage accounts, and crypto wallets to an AI tax optimization system after a sleepless night spent estimating her next tax bill. She expected better tracking. What she got was perspective. The AI did something no advisor had ever done before. It showed her a timeline. Not a spreadsheet, not a form — a living projection of her financial future. Every year was mapped out with estimated income, deductions, gains, losses, and taxes. For the first time, Sarah saw how one decision echoed across decades.

The system highlighted a painful truth. Her biggest crypto gains had always occurred in the same years her rental income peaked. She was stacking taxable income without realizing it. Meanwhile, her best real estate depreciation years had gone partially unused because they did not align with her highest income periods. Nothing was coordinated. Everything was accidental.

The AI proposed a different approach. It suggested harvesting certain crypto losses in the current year to offset rental income. It recommended delaying a property sale by twelve months to allow depreciation to fully shelter a future stock liquidation. It even suggested adjusting dividend reinvestment timing to avoid unnecessary bracket creep.

At first, Sarah hesitated. The plan required patience. It required trust. But the projections were clear. The difference between her current path and the optimized path was staggering — not just in taxes saved, but in net worth preserved.

She followed the strategy.

Throughout the year, Sarah checked the AI dashboard regularly. It updated in real time. When markets dipped, the AI adjusted. When income rose unexpectedly, it rebalanced the plan. Every move felt intentional, coordinated, calm.

Tax season arrived — and for the first time in her adult life, Sarah felt no dread. Her tax bill was lower than any year she could remember, despite earning more. Even better, the AI showed her that she had positioned herself perfectly for the years ahead. Losses were banked. Depreciation was aligned. Gains were timed.

That night, Sarah sat at her kitchen table, not with stacks of papers, but with a sense of clarity. She realized that wealth was never about picking the perfect investment. It was about making sure every investment worked together.

The year everything finally clicked was not the year she earned the most money. It was the year she stopped fighting the system and started using intelligence to shape it. And from that point on, her wealth no longer felt fragile. It felt inevitable.

Chapter 6

How AI Prevents Tax Disasters, Audits & Costly Compliance Mistakes

Most tax damage does not come from aggressive behavior. It comes from small, invisible mistakes that compound quietly over time. Missed forms, misclassified income, incorrect cost basis, unreported wallets, misunderstood passive loss rules, or poorly timed sales often trigger penalties, audits, and permanent loss of deductions. Investors rarely realize the danger until years later, when the IRS sends a notice that reopens the past. Artificial intelligence exists not only to optimize taxes, but to prevent these disasters before they ever occur.

The modern tax environment is unforgiving. Real estate investors must comply with depreciation rules, recapture calculations, passive activity limitations, material participation tests, and reporting obligations that vary by state and property type. Crypto investors must track every transaction across wallets, exchanges, bridges, DeFi platforms, NFTs, and staking protocols, often retroactively. Investment accounts introduce wash sale rules, dividend classifications, and capital gains timing issues. The sheer volume of rules makes error inevitable without intelligent automation.

AI changes compliance from reactive to preventative. Instead of reviewing transactions after the fact, AI watches them as they happen. It flags potential issues in real time. If a crypto transaction lacks cost basis, AI reconstructs it. If a real estate expense is miscategorized, AI corrects it. If an action would violate a tax rule, AI warns you before execution. This preemptive intelligence eliminates the most dangerous category of tax risk: unintentional noncompliance.

Audit risk is not random. Certain behaviors, patterns, and inconsistencies dramatically increase the likelihood of scrutiny. Large unexplained losses, mismatched income reporting, inconsistent depreciation schedules, incomplete crypto disclosures, and sudden swings in deductions all attract attention. AI understands these patterns. It analyzes your filings the same way regulators do, identifying anomalies and smoothing risk before returns are ever submitted.

One of the most powerful features of AI-driven compliance is documentation. Audits are not won by explanations — they are won by evidence. AI automatically stores transaction histories, depreciation schedules, cost segregation logic, activity logs, and supporting documentation in organized, retrievable formats. If questions arise years later, the evidence is already prepared. This turns audits from stressful ordeals into structured reviews. AI also adapts as laws change. Tax regulations evolve constantly, especially in emerging areas like crypto and digital assets. What was acceptable last year may be penalized this year. AI systems are updated continuously, applying new rules automatically and retroactively adjusting projections. This protects investors from relying on outdated advice or assumptions that no longer apply.

Another hidden danger AI eliminates is overconfidence. Many investors assume their accountant is catching everything. In reality, even skilled professionals rely on the data they are given. If something is missing or misreported upstream, errors propagate downstream. AI does not rely on assumptions. It cross-checks sources, reconciles discrepancies, and validates completeness automatically.

Perhaps the most valuable outcome of AI-driven compliance is peace of mind. Investors who understand their tax position clearly make better decisions. They take opportunities they would otherwise avoid. They reinvest with confidence. They stop hoarding cash out of fear. Compliance becomes invisible — not because it is ignored, but because it is handled continuously and intelligently.

This chapter represents the final evolution of AI-powered tax strategy. Optimization increases wealth. Coordination accelerates compounding. But protection preserves everything you have built. AI ensures that success does not become a liability, and that growth does not invite unnecessary risk. When compliance is automated and proactive, wealth becomes resilient.

"The Letter That Never Came"

For most of his investing life, Daniel lived with a quiet fear he never admitted out loud. It followed him through property closings, crypto trades, and brokerage statements. Every April, it whispered the same question: *What did I miss this time?*

Daniel was successful by most standards. He owned multiple rental properties, traded crypto actively, and maintained a growing investment portfolio. But his financial life was messy. Wallets scattered across platforms. Properties managed by different systems. Investments tracked in fragments. He trusted that his accountant would sort it all out in the end.

Then one spring afternoon, a friend called him in a panic.

The IRS had opened an audit. Three years back. Crypto discrepancies. Missing cost basis. Penalties stacking fast.

That night, Daniel couldn't sleep.

He replayed every transaction he had ever made, every wallet he had forgotten, every trade he couldn't quite explain anymore. He imagined envelopes arriving, deadlines ticking, explanations failing. He realized the most dangerous thing about taxes was not what you did wrong — it was what you didn't even know you had done.

The next morning, Daniel connected everything to an AI tax intelligence platform.

At first, the system said nothing. It simply worked.

It ingested years of data. It mapped his entire financial history. It rebuilt transactions he had forgotten. It flagged inconsistencies quietly, methodically, without judgment. When the dashboard finally appeared, Daniel felt something he hadn't felt in years: clarity.

The AI showed him where risks had existed — and where they no longer did. It identified transactions that could have caused problems and showed how they had been resolved. It highlighted areas where documentation was thin and generated supporting records automatically. It corrected depreciation schedules. It aligned reporting across accounts.

Most importantly, it simulated how his return would look through the eyes of an auditor.

No red flags. No anomalies.

No unexplained gaps.

Over the next year, Daniel changed how he operated. He stopped guessing. He stopped assuming. Before every major decision, the AI evaluated compliance impact alongside profit. When crypto rules changed, the system updated instantly. When he renovated a property, documentation appeared automatically. When he considered selling an asset, the AI showed both tax optimization and audit exposure side by side.

Tax season arrived.

Daniel waited.

No letters.

No notices.

No corrections.

Weeks passed. Then months.

The letter that never came became the greatest confirmation of all.

Years later, Daniel realized that wealth wasn't just about making the right moves. It was about protecting the past while building the future. The AI hadn't just saved him money – it had saved him from uncertainty.

And in a world where success often attracts scrutiny, that quiet protection was worth more than any return he had ever earned.

Chapter 7

How AI Builds a Long-Term Exit, Legacy & Wealth-Preservation Tax Strategy

Most investors focus on how to acquire assets. Very few plan for how to exit them. This is one of the most expensive mistakes in wealth building. Taxes are not just triggered when income is earned — they are often largest when assets are sold, transferred, inherited, or restructured. Artificial intelligence transforms exit planning from a reactive event into a long-term, continuously optimized strategy that protects wealth across decades and generations.

An exit is not a single moment. It is a sequence of decisions made years in advance. Selling a property, unwinding a crypto position, liquidating a portfolio, transferring ownership to family members, or repositioning assets for retirement all have cascading tax consequences. Humans tend to make these decisions emotionally or under time pressure. AI removes emotion and urgency by modeling outcomes far ahead of time.

Artificial intelligence continuously evaluates when, how, and whether assets should be sold at all. It compares selling versus refinancing. It weighs exchanging versus holding. It analyzes stepped-up basis implications, depreciation recapture timing, capital gains exposure, and future income projections. It shows investors that sometimes the most profitable exit is no exit at all — but a strategic repositioning.

For real estate investors, AI models generational strategies. It understands how depreciation shields income today while stepped-up basis can erase gains tomorrow. It identifies when holding property until inheritance produces exponentially better outcomes than selling during life. It coordinates gifting strategies, trusts, and ownership structures to minimize estate and capital gains taxes simultaneously. What once required elite estate planners is now accessible through intelligent automation.

Crypto and digital assets add urgency to exit planning. Regulatory frameworks are evolving, reporting requirements are tightening, and tax treatment continues to shift. AI monitors regulatory changes and models future scenarios, helping investors unwind positions gradually, harvest gains strategically, or reposition assets into more tax-efficient structures. This proactive planning prevents forced exits driven by fear or compliance pressure.

AI also integrates retirement timing into tax exits. Many investors unknowingly liquidate assets at peak tax exposure just before retirement, missing opportunities to spread gains into lower-income years. AI models income trajectories, Social Security timing, required minimum distributions, and asset drawdown strategies. It aligns exits with life phases rather than calendar years.

Legacy planning becomes radically more precise with AI. Instead of vague intentions, investors see exact outcomes. They see how much wealth transfers intact. They see which assets should be sold, held, gifted, or restructured. They see how tax drag compounds over generations — and how intelligent planning eliminates it. Wealth preservation stops being abstract and becomes measurable.

Perhaps the most powerful role AI plays in exit strategy is patience. It shows the cost of rushing. It quantifies the benefit of waiting. It demonstrates how one extra year of planning can save decades of erosion. When investors can see the future clearly, they stop sabotaging it.

This chapter represents the final stage of AI-powered tax mastery. Acquisition builds wealth. Optimization accelerates it. Protection preserves it. Exit strategy ensures it lasts. Artificial intelligence connects all four into a single, enduring system — one that turns temporary success into permanent legacy.

"The Last Sale"

Everyone assumed Michael would sell.

He owned eight rental properties, a diversified crypto portfolio, and investment accounts that had grown steadily for over twenty years. Friends told him it was time. Markets were strong. Prices were high. He was nearing retirement. The logic seemed obvious.

But something didn't feel right.

Michael had spent his life building assets patiently, deliberately. The idea of unwinding everything in a rush made him uneasy. Not because he feared the market – but because he feared making a decision he didn't fully understand.

Late one evening, he connected his entire financial life to an AI tax intelligence system he had been quietly evaluating. He expected projections. What he got was perspective.

The AI did not start with numbers. It started with questions.

What does success look like to you at age seventy? At eighty? What do you want to leave behind? How much control do you want to keep? How much certainty do you need?

Michael answered honestly. Then the system worked.

It modeled selling everything immediately. The tax bill was staggering. Capital gains, depreciation recapture, state taxes – decades of work evaporated in a single transaction. The net number on the screen made his stomach tighten.

Then it modeled a second scenario.

Refinance instead of sell. Use depreciation to shelter remaining income. Harvest crypto gains gradually. Defer real estate exits. Coordinate drawdowns with retirement income. Let time do the work.

The difference was shocking.

In the optimized path, Michael never sold most of his properties. He refinanced strategically, pulling out tax-free capital. He reduced income gradually as he transitioned into retirement, keeping himself in lower brackets. Crypto positions were unwound over several years, offset by losses and deductions the AI had been quietly tracking.

Then the AI showed him something he had never fully considered.

Legacy.

It modeled what would happen if he held certain properties until death. The stepped-up basis erased decades of unrealized gains. His heirs would inherit clean assets — not tax bombs. The wealth he had built would transfer almost intact.

Michael stared at the screen for a long time.

Selling had always felt like the finish line. Now he saw it differently. Selling was just one option — and often the most expensive one.

Over the next few years, Michael followed the AI's guidance with calm discipline. He ignored market noise. He ignored pressure. Every move was deliberate. Every decision aligned with a future he could finally see clearly.

When he eventually sold his final property — years later than anyone expected — the transaction felt quiet, almost ceremonial. The taxes were manageable. The impact was controlled. Nothing felt rushed or regretted.

One evening, sitting on his porch as the sun dipped low, Michael realized something profound.

The most powerful decision he had ever made wasn't what to buy.

It was knowing exactly how — and when — to let go.

And thanks to intelligence that could see further than he ever could alone, the last sale wasn't an ending at all. It was simply the moment his wealth became permanent.

Chapter 8

How AI Adapts to Changing Tax Laws, Markets & Life Events Automatically

One of the most dangerous assumptions investors make is believing that the rules they learned last year will still apply next year. Tax law is not static. Markets are not predictable. Life does not move in straight lines. Marriage, divorce, children, relocation, career shifts, health events, market crashes, regulatory changes, and political cycles all reshape tax outcomes — often overnight. Artificial intelligence exists to operate in this uncertainty, adapting continuously so your tax strategy never becomes outdated or fragile.

Traditional tax planning is frozen in time. A CPA reviews past activity, applies rules as they existed, and files a return based on what already happened. But the most expensive tax mistakes occur between filing seasons, when decisions are made using old assumptions in a changing world. AI replaces static planning with living intelligence. It recalibrates constantly as laws change, markets move, and your personal circumstances evolve.

Tax law alone changes at a pace that humans struggle to track. Depreciation rules are expanded or rolled back. Bonus depreciation phases in and out. Crypto reporting requirements tighten. Information returns increase. New disclosures appear. Thresholds shift. Safe harbors change. Artificial intelligence systems ingest regulatory updates as they occur, automatically updating calculations, projections, and compliance logic. What was optimal yesterday is reevaluated today — without requiring you to relearn the system.

Market volatility compounds this complexity. A sudden market downturn can create loss-harvesting opportunities. A rapid bull market can push income into higher brackets. Interest rate changes affect refinancing decisions. Real estate cycles alter depreciation and exit strategies. AI monitors these shifts continuously, adjusting recommendations in real time. It treats volatility not as chaos, but as raw data.

Life events are where most tax strategies quietly fail. A move to a new state can change tax exposure dramatically. A change in filing status can invalidate assumptions. A new business or investment can alter eligibility for deductions. A sudden inheritance can introduce estate considerations. AI systems incorporate life events into their models immediately, recalculating strategies across every asset and future year.

One of AI's greatest strengths is resilience. Instead of building a strategy that only works if everything goes according to plan,

AI builds adaptive systems that survive disruption. It stress-tests your tax strategy against worst-case scenarios and upside scenarios alike. It shows how strategies hold up under different income levels, market conditions, and legal frameworks. This transforms tax planning from fragile optimization into durable engineering.

AI also protects against emotional decision-making during change. Humans react to fear, excitement, and pressure. AI reacts to data. When markets crash, AI identifies opportunity instead of panic. When income spikes, AI manages exposure instead of celebration. When laws change, AI recalculates instead of resisting. This emotional neutrality preserves wealth when humans are most likely to make irreversible mistakes.

Another overlooked benefit of adaptability is longevity. A strategy that works for five years but fails in year six can destroy decades of progress. AI builds strategies that evolve as you age, as your goals shift, and as your financial ecosystem grows. It transitions you smoothly from accumulation to preservation, from growth to income, from ownership to legacy — without abrupt tax shocks.

In a world defined by uncertainty, adaptability is the ultimate advantage. Artificial intelligence ensures that your tax strategy is never locked into the past. It moves forward with you, adjusting silently, continuously, and intelligently. Instead of fearing change, you benefit from it.

This chapter represents the difference between optimization and durability. AI does not just help you win today. It helps you remain optimized no matter what tomorrow brings.

"The Year Everything Changed Twice"

If anyone had asked Lena to describe her life at the start of the year, she would have used one word: stable.

She owned four rental properties, held a long-term crypto portfolio, and worked as a consultant earning steady income. Her tax strategy felt settled. Predictable. Safe. She believed she finally understood how her financial world worked.

Then everything changed.

The first shift came quietly. A new client doubled her income almost overnight. What felt like a victory quickly turned into anxiety when Lena realized she was heading toward the highest tax bracket she had ever faced. Old assumptions crumbled. Deductions that once mattered now felt small. She felt successful — and exposed.

A month later, markets shifted. Crypto surged unexpectedly, pushing unrealized gains into numbers she had never seen before. Friends urged her to sell. Headlines screamed opportunity. Lena hesitated, unsure whether acting would help or hurt her long-term position.

Then came the third change — the one she never saw coming.

Her father passed away suddenly, leaving behind property, accounts, and unfinished plans. Grief collided with complexity. Questions surfaced faster than answers. What to keep. What to sell. What to transfer. What to protect.

In previous years, Lena would have been overwhelmed. This time, she had something different.

She opened her AI tax intelligence system.

The dashboard had already changed.

Her increased income had been incorporated automatically. Brackets recalculated. Withholding projections adjusted. The system had already flagged a strategy to defer income and accelerate deductions to soften the impact. What could have been a shock had become manageable.

Crypto projections updated next. The AI showed multiple paths — sell now and pay heavily, hold and risk volatility, or unwind gradually while offsetting gains using losses and depreciation. The numbers were clear. The emotion faded.

Then the inheritance appeared on the screen.

The AI integrated it calmly, respectfully. It modeled stepped-up basis outcomes. It showed which assets were best held, which could be sold tax-efficiently, and which should be transferred intact. It coordinated everything with Lena's existing portfolio instead of treating it as a disruption.

For the first time since her father's death, Lena felt grounded.

As the year unfolded, changes continued. Laws shifted. Markets dipped. Income stabilized. Each time, the AI adapted. Recommendations evolved. Projections adjusted. No panic. No scrambling. No surprises.

By year's end, Lena sat quietly reviewing her tax summary. Despite earning more, inheriting assets, and navigating volatile markets, her tax exposure was controlled. Her future projections looked stronger than ever. What could have been a financial disaster had become a turning point.

She realized something then.

The most valuable thing the AI had given her wasn't savings.

It was stability in motion. Life would change again. Markets would shift again. Laws would evolve again. But now, Lena understood that she didn't need certainty to move forward.

She needed intelligence that could move with her.

And in a year where everything changed twice – and then again – that adaptability had made all the difference.

Chapter 9

How AI Turns Tax Strategy Into a Permanent Wealth-Building System

Most people believe tax planning is something you do. In reality, effective tax strategy is something you *build*. It is not a checklist, a one-time optimization, or a clever deduction discovered at the last minute. It is a system — one that must operate continuously, intelligently, and without interruption. Artificial intelligence transforms tax strategy from a temporary effort into a permanent wealth-building engine that compounds alongside your investments.

Traditional tax planning resets every year. You file. You forget. You repeat. Each cycle starts from scratch, relying on memory, manual inputs, and outdated assumptions. This approach guarantees inefficiency because wealth itself does not reset annually. Assets compound. Income streams evolve. Decisions echo forward. AI closes this gap by creating continuity — a single system that remembers everything, learns from every decision, and improves over time.

When AI manages your tax strategy, every action feeds the system. Each investment, transaction, and life event becomes data that sharpens future recommendations. Over time, AI learns your patterns, risk tolerance, goals, and behavior. It does not just apply tax rules — it applies *your* strategy consistently across years, assets, and situations. This is how tax planning becomes infrastructure instead of effort.

One of the most powerful effects of systemized tax strategy is compounding efficiency. Small improvements repeated over decades create enormous outcomes. A few percentage points saved each year do not simply add up — they multiply. AI ensures those savings are not lost due to oversight, fatigue, or complexity. It executes relentlessly, preserving marginal gains that humans would inevitably miss.

AI also eliminates strategic drift. Many investors begin with clear intentions but gradually abandon them as complexity grows. New assets are added without integration. Old assumptions linger after circumstances change. AI prevents this by constantly aligning decisions with the overarching system. It ensures that growth does not erode coherence and that success does not create chaos.

Another critical advantage of AI-driven systems is scalability. As portfolios grow, traditional planning becomes less effective. Complexity increases faster than human capacity. AI scales effortlessly. Whether you manage five assets or five hundred, the system applies the same precision. Growth becomes safer, not riskier.

This permanence also changes behavior. Investors who trust their tax system take smarter risks. They reinvest confidently. They avoid hoarding cash out of fear. They pursue opportunity without anxiety. Wealth accelerates not because they work harder, but because friction has been removed.

Perhaps the most overlooked benefit of AI as a permanent system is generational continuity. Most wealth is lost not through poor investing, but through poor transitions. Knowledge disappears. Strategies are forgotten. Heirs start over. AI preserves institutional memory. It documents reasoning, decisions, and structure so wealth can persist beyond the original builder.

By the time you reach this chapter, one truth should be clear: taxes are not the enemy of wealth. Disorganization is. Artificial intelligence replaces chaos with structure, randomness with intention, and effort with automation. It ensures that every dollar you earn, save, and invest works in harmony with the rest.

This is the moment tax planning stops being something you think about — and becomes something that simply works.

"The Quiet Advantage"

No one ever thought of Thomas as extraordinary.

He didn't chase headlines. He didn't brag about deals. He didn't post screenshots of gains or argue about markets. If anything, Thomas seemed almost boring — methodical, calm, predictable.

But over twenty years, something strange happened.

Thomas quietly became wealthy.

Not overnight. Not explosively. Gradually. Inevitably.

When colleagues compared notes, Thomas's returns didn't look dramatically higher. His properties weren't flashier. His investments weren't riskier. Yet his net worth kept pulling away from everyone else's.

The difference wasn't what he bought.

It was what he kept.

Early in his investing life, Thomas made a decision that felt unremarkable at the time. He connected his finances to an AI-driven tax intelligence system and committed to letting it run — year after year — without interference. At first, the changes were subtle. Slightly lower tax bills. Cleaner records.

Better timing. Nothing dramatic. Friends chased higher yields. Thomas ignored the noise.

Then time did its work.

As years passed, the system grew more intelligent. It remembered past decisions. It refined strategies. It learned how Thomas invested, how his income fluctuated, how markets affected him emotionally. It adjusted automatically.

When Thomas bought new properties, they integrated seamlessly. When he experimented with crypto, risk was controlled. When markets surged, gains were managed. When downturns came, losses were harvested. Nothing felt reactive. Everything felt intentional.

Thomas noticed something else too.

He was never stressed at tax time.

While others scrambled, second-guessed, and panicked, Thomas simply reviewed a summary. The work had already been done — continuously, quietly, invisibly.

Years later, when Thomas reduced his workload, the system adjusted. Income declined smoothly. Brackets optimized. Drawdowns coordinated. Retirement arrived not as a cliff, but as a gentle slope.

Eventually, his children became curious.

"How did you always know what to do?" they asked.

Thomas smiled.

"I didn't," he said. "I built something that did."

When Thomas passed, his family expected complexity. Instead, they found clarity. Documentation. Structure. A system that explained itself. The AI guided transitions, minimized taxes, preserved value. Nothing unraveled.

Years later, one of Thomas's children reflected on what they had inherited.

It wasn't just money.

It was continuity.

The quiet advantage wasn't brilliance or luck.

It was permanence.

And that permanence — built patiently, protected intelligently, and allowed to run uninterrupted — had done what no single decision ever could.

It had made wealth inevitable.

Chapter 10

The AI-Powered Future of Personal Tax Optimization

The future of personal taxation will not be defined by forms, deadlines, or last-minute scrambling. It will be defined by systems that operate continuously, invisibly, and intelligently in the background of everyday life. Artificial intelligence is not simply improving how taxes are prepared — it is fundamentally redefining how individuals interact with the tax system itself. What was once reactive is becoming proactive. What was once confusing is becoming transparent. What was once stressful is becoming automated.

In the traditional world, taxes were something that happened *to* you. You earned income, made investments, lived your life, and then waited to be told what you owed. AI reverses this relationship. Taxes become something that responds to *you* in real time. Every financial decision is evaluated instantly for tax impact. Every opportunity is surfaced before it expires. Every risk is flagged before it becomes a problem. This shift turns taxation from a punitive afterthought into a strategic design layer of personal finance. As AI continues to evolve, tax optimization will no longer be limited to calculations. It will incorporate behavioral modeling, predictive analytics, and scenario forecasting at a level no human advisor can replicate. AI will anticipate how future laws may affect current decisions. It will model multiple political, economic, and regulatory outcomes simultaneously. It will recommend strategies that are robust not just under one future, but under many possible futures.

Personal tax systems will increasingly resemble operating systems rather than tools. They will integrate income, spending, investing, insurance, estate planning, and compliance into a unified framework. Instead of managing dozens of apps, statements, and advisors, individuals will rely on a single intelligent layer that understands how everything fits together. Taxes will no longer interrupt life — they will flow with it.

Another defining feature of the AI-powered future is personalization at scale. Two people earning the same income will receive completely different strategies based on their goals, risk tolerance, family structure, geography, and timeline. AI does not offer generic advice. It tailors optimization continuously, adjusting as life evolves. This eliminates the one-size-fits-all limitations that have plagued traditional tax planning for generations.

The future will also bring radical transparency. Instead of vague estimates and confusing projections, individuals will see clear, visual representations of how decisions affect long-term outcomes. They will understand not just *what* to do, but *why* it matters. Financial literacy will no longer depend on years of experience — it will be embedded directly into intelligent systems that explain themselves.

Perhaps most importantly, AI will democratize what was once reserved for the ultra-wealthy. Complex strategies involving timing, coordination, and long-term planning will become accessible to anyone willing to adopt intelligent systems. This will not eliminate inequality overnight, but it will remove one of the greatest structural disadvantages: lack of access to sophisticated financial intelligence.

In this future, compliance will be automatic. Audits will be rare. Errors will be detected before filings occur. Reporting will happen continuously rather than annually. The relationship between individuals and tax authorities will shift from adversarial to procedural. Taxes will feel less like a threat and more like infrastructure.

What this ultimately creates is freedom. Freedom from fear. Freedom from uncertainty. Freedom from wasted effort. Individuals will spend less time managing money and more time living their lives — confident that their financial system is working intelligently on their behalf.

This is not a distant vision. It is already happening. And those who adopt AI-powered tax optimization early will experience a compounding advantage that extends far beyond money. They will gain clarity, confidence, and control — not just over their taxes, but over their financial futures.

The era of reactive taxation is ending. The era of intelligent, automated, and personalized tax strategy has begun.

"The System That Outlived Him"

When Julian first built his financial system, he didn't think of it as something permanent.

He was in his early forties, busy, ambitious, and focused on growth. Taxes were an annoyance — something to be handled efficiently and forgotten. He adopted an AI-driven tax optimization platform because it promised automation and savings, not because he was thinking about legacy.

At first, the system felt almost invisible.

It categorized transactions quietly. It optimized timing without fanfare. It adjusted projections silently as markets moved.

Julian noticed lower tax bills and fewer surprises, but life went on much the same.

Years passed.

Julian acquired properties. Sold a few. Entered new investments. Tried crypto. Exited some positions. Changed states. Started a business. Sold that too. Through every transition, the system adapted without complaint or confusion. It recalculated. It restructured. It remembered.

Julian began to trust it deeply.

While others panicked during market crashes, Julian reviewed calm projections. While friends celebrated big wins only to dread tax season, Julian already knew the outcome months in advance. The system didn't make him richer overnight — it made him steadier.

As Julian aged, priorities shifted. Growth mattered less than preservation. Income mattered more than accumulation. The system noticed before he did. It began recommending different strategies — fewer aggressive moves, more stability, smoother transitions. Julian followed along, grateful for the clarity.

One winter, Julian became ill.

At first, it seemed temporary. But time proved otherwise. As treatments progressed, financial decisions faded into the background. Julian trusted the system to handle what he no longer had energy to manage.

When Julian passed, his family expected chaos.

Instead, they found order.

Every asset was mapped. Every decision documented. Every strategy explained. The AI guided transitions calmly — which assets to hold, which to sell, how to minimize taxes, how to preserve value. Nothing unraveled. Nothing was lost.

Julian's children learned more about their father through the system than they ever had through conversation. They saw his patience in the way strategies unfolded over decades. They saw his values reflected in the choices preserved. They saw a life not just lived, but *designed.*

Years later, long after Julian was gone, the system still ran.

It adjusted to new laws. It adapted to new markets. It guided new decisions for a new generation. The intelligence he had put in place outlived him — quietly continuing the work he had started.

One evening, Julian's eldest child reviewed the projections and realized something profound.

The greatest gift Julian had left behind wasn't money.

It was continuity.

A system that didn't forget.

A system that didn't panic.

A system that turned intention into permanence.

And in that quiet persistence, Julian's influence endured — not as memory alone, but as intelligence still shaping the future.

Final Thoughts

The End of Tax Guesswork—and the Beginning of Intelligent Wealth

For most of modern history, taxes have been treated as an unavoidable burden — a necessary cost of success, something to be minimized when possible and endured when not. Investors learned to accept uncertainty, surprises, and inefficiency as part of the process. They planned investments first and dealt with taxes later, often discovering too late that the decisions they made in pursuit of growth quietly eroded their long-term wealth. This book was written to challenge that assumption and to offer a different future — one where intelligence replaces guesswork and strategy replaces reaction.

Artificial intelligence marks the first time in history that individuals can manage taxes with the same sophistication, foresight, and precision once reserved exclusively for institutions and ultra-wealthy families. Throughout this book, you have seen how AI transforms every stage of the tax lifecycle — from tracking and compliance to optimization, coordination, protection, adaptation, and ultimately legacy. These are not isolated features. Together, they form a complete system for preserving wealth over time.

The most important realization is this: taxes are not a one-time problem to be solved, but a continuous force that shapes outcomes year after year. Every decision — buying, selling, holding, trading, refinancing, gifting, inheriting — leaves a tax footprint that compounds across time. Without a system that understands this continuity, even the best investment strategies eventually leak value. AI closes that gap by creating memory, structure, and foresight where none existed before.

This book has shown that tax optimization is not about finding loopholes or taking reckless positions. It is about alignment. Alignment between assets. Alignment between timing and income. Alignment between laws and incentives. Alignment between present actions and future outcomes. Artificial intelligence excels at alignment because it sees the entire system at once — not just isolated transactions or single-year results.

One of the greatest myths in personal finance is that complexity is a disadvantage. In truth, complexity is only dangerous when it is unmanaged. When guided by intelligence, complexity becomes opportunity. Real estate depreciation, capital gains timing, loss harvesting, coordinated exits, adaptive compliance — these are not burdens. They are levers. AI allows you to pull them intentionally instead of stumbling into them accidentally. Another theme that runs through this book is resilience. Markets change. Laws evolve. Life events disrupt even the best-laid plans. Traditional tax strategies often fail because they are rigid — optimized for a single scenario that rarely unfolds exactly as expected. AI-powered systems are different. They are designed to adapt. They stress-test decisions, recalibrate projections, and evolve alongside your life. This adaptability is not a luxury; it is the foundation of long-term success.

Perhaps the most profound shift AI creates is psychological. Fear fades when clarity exists. Confidence replaces hesitation. Investors stop avoiding opportunity out of uncertainty and stop overreacting to volatility. With AI providing continuous insight, decisions become calmer, slower, and more deliberate. Wealth grows not because risk increases, but because friction disappears.

As you close this book, it is important to understand that adopting AI-powered tax optimization is not about chasing the future — it is about protecting your time, your energy, and your attention. The greatest cost of inefficient taxes is not money alone. It is stress. It is distraction. It is the mental weight of uncertainty. AI removes that weight by handling complexity quietly in the background, allowing you to focus on building the life you actually want.

The future of personal taxation will belong to those who build systems, not those who rely on memory or luck. It will belong to those who understand that wealth is not just earned — it is preserved, coordinated, and transferred intentionally. Artificial intelligence is the tool that makes this possible at scale.

You now have the framework. The next step is implementation. Connect your assets. Trust the system. Let intelligence compound alongside your investments. Over time, the results will speak for themselves — quietly, predictably, and powerfully.

The era of reactive taxation is over. The era of intelligent wealth has begun.

www.ingramcontent.com/pod-product-compliance
Lightning Source LLC
LaVergne TN
LVHW022024200926
848481LV00007B/2520
* 9 7 9 8 2 9 5 5 8 6 0 5 7 *